OUTSIDE THE WIRE

A U.S. Marine's Collection of
Combat Poems & Short Stories

by
Justin T. Eggen

Untitled

ii

For Nimish
and
To the Marines we lost in
Operation Enduring Freedom

SGT Trevor J. Johnson
SGT David W. Wallace
CPL Anthony L. Williams
LCPL Jonathon F. Stroud
LCPL Omar G.D. Roebuck
CPL Jacob H. Turbett
LCPL Alejandro Yazzie
SGT Jeremy R. McQueary
LCPL Larry M. Johnson
CPL Joseph C. Whitehead
SSGT Jason A. Rogers
LCPL Ronald D. Freeman
LCPL Joshua B. McDaniels
LCPL Robert S. Greniger
LCPL Franklin N. Watson
SSGT David H. Stewart
CPL Brandon J. Garabrant
CPL Adam F. Wolff

This collection is dedicated to you.

Follow Me, Tread Lightly

FOREWORD

When I moved back to Florida after being gone for over four full years, it felt like I had been gone for a decade. Remnants of my old life were sparse, and things were different, although somehow the same. I really knew only two things: the Marine Corps and Afghanistan, and I didn't know how I was going to transition back into this life, or if I even could.

I had spent years focusing on one thing, doing one job, and evolving into this person. I became someone who was prepared for the worst possible outcomes in life with the means to handle them. I've been home five years now, yet these thoughts still persist daily. Even as I write this foreword, my mind is constantly anxious, waiting for that whistle from the indirect fire or that shudder in your lungs from the deep boom of the I.E.D. I'm often reminded of the loss and struggle we went through as a generation. It is my opinion that most service members who served in the Middle East might feel this way.

The years went on, and I suppressed a majority of my memories from overseas. I only let in the safe ones, the ones that weren't traumatic. This was a toxic way of living, to say the least. I was carrying this weight in my mind that was heavier than any physical object. I couldn't stand to suppress those memories and traumatic events, hoping they wouldn't rise up to take over my brain. I was exhausting myself by doing this.

I tried to have relationships and live a "normal" life but failed. I couldn't really live my life without letting these memories show themselves. I had to accept them, accept the things that had happened, and accept the reality. Letting them live with the rest of my memories seemed to be the only means for my mind to really level out.

Combat is terrifying. It's beautiful, it's devastating, and unrelenting. There is something so simple about being in the middle of it. When you're there in the middle of the daily shit storms, you can't think about anything but doing your job and focusing on staying alive. On downtime you think about home, the first night back with your girl, eating the foods you love, daily showers, and your daily bathroom routines you miss so much.

When I stepped off the bus coming home from my final deployment, something happened. I was hit with a wave of depression and emotions, knowing I'd made it back. Everything hit me at once, and I didn't know how to actually absorb it. I took that feeling and suppressed it along with every single fucked-up situation that ever happened overseas and never thought twice about it.

After being home a few months, I had already tried to commit suicide on my twenty-third birthday, which seemingly ended my marriage. My life in the Marine Corps was coming to an end, and I had no purpose at this point in my life. As far as I had been concerned, once I left North Carolina, my life would be a million times better. But it wasn't.

I had some great times after moving back to Florida, but in December 2014, I was riding my '08 Harley Davidson Dyna Streetbob down the road about 50 mph, and was T-boned by a car. I was ejected from my bike by an eighty-seven-year-old man pulling out of a living community. I saw him pulling out and silently thought, "Please don't pull out in front of me, please," but sure enough, just as I got in front of him, he pulled out.

I was physically okay afterward, just a fractured ankle and road rash covering my back. The mental pain was there instantly, and remains until this day. When I drive down any road and someone

vi

looks like they're about to pull out into traffic, I expect it. I fear it. My mind thinks I'm going to get hit again. It's something minor I live with and try to ignore, but I just can't.

The same thing happens to me regarding Afghanistan. It's just something I cannot ignore. The memories I suppressed the day I returned home have eaten away at my soul. Writing has been a way to share them; it's forced me to relive them and forced me to be okay with them. This book is evidence that you can channel your traumatic memories into something beautiful.

I started writing poetry when I was young, and it has stuck with me until now. It's healthy for me. It cleans my mind out. My poetry is a way for me to release a lot of the darker, more extreme events. I'm trying to force the reader to really read the poems and see them for the dark, gritty, and combat-oriented poetry that it is. That's why I call them "Combat Poems." The short stories are more of a way to bring the softer side of the battlefield to the readers.

This book isn't a memoir. It is a dark collection of deep poetry and short stories that show a different perspective.

No one carries this pain alone.
It's on all of us.
We are in it together.
We have each other.

TABLE OF CONTENTS

Opposition Grows

We find them with sight.
Each patrol leads to new
   plight.
Step on one, you're done.

Low orders are few
And far between these alleys,
   Exchanging volleys.

We win battles here,
Fusillade to suppress foes.
Opposition grows.

BOOK 1
★

I'm the Enemy

Battling my soul,
I'm the enemy inside.
Fighting takes its toll.

Consumed

At war with myself,
Things change. Life is
different.
Anger, hate consume.

Monuments

Everything at cost,
Wall of sacrifice shows loss,
Monuments see frost

Suicide Poem

Shooting myself would be easy.
I know it would hurt, and I
know it's selfish.
That doesn't change the fact
that I don't want to die yet.
At the same time, I died a long
time ago.
So what's the harm
in suck starting a forty-five,
when everything around you
seems pointless?
We lose people every day,
And every day we mourn,
So why not have people mourn
me?

It's the will to live and push
through the bullshit and bring
yourself to the side of
happiness.

This side is the light side, full
of joy, charisma, and elation.
Real euphoria.
Full of family, friends,
companions, lovers, and life.
The kind of happiness that
pushes you
To continue living on this
beautiful planet,
The kind of paradise that
brightens the darkest days.
The kind of perfection you
realize is there halfway into
writing your suicide poem.

The light is there.
Everyone is there.
We are here.

Night Terrors

Night terrors approach.
Dark, vast, expansive dreams
  loom.
My mind fills with doom.

Nightmares You Fight

Tourniquets tightened,
Your eyes only will find it.
Nightmares—you fight it.

She Smiles, She Speaks

I can't sleep.
Where am I?
Did I wake?
No,
I have no gear,
No purpose.
What is this?
It's cold,
It's black.
Why?
I feel it—
Death.
I turn and see.
Her face is gentle.
She smiles, she speaks:
"One day,
Soon."
She backs up.
"Why did you come?"
There is no reply.

So Close

You become humbled.
Death was so close, within
reach.
Never fear stumbles.

Taken from Me

Compassion fails me,
    Taken from me overseas.
        I'm home and broken.

Will of Combat

Never blame yourself.
It was the will of combat.
You will always hurt.

None

Here we find our fate.
Time consumes you after war,
Knowing none relate.

Death Follows

Death follows like a shadow,
Wives become widows,
Stepping on pressure plates
  daily.
Low orders are seldom.

Like a Dream

Marjah, Sangin, both,
Like a dream we shared in
time,
Relived in our minds.

From Within

Realities end,
New beginnings will begin—
Death comes from within.

Minutes Turn into Weeks

It doesn't let you leave.
The bond seeps when you
bleed,
Forever ingrained in your soul,
The memories relentlessly
taking their toll.
Minutes turn into weeks.
My mind doesn't want to sleep.
The soul can't take much more
of this.
My mind is heavy, and it needs
rest,
Never sleeping, only awake.
My memories must go away.

Life

Explosions erupt.
Bodies are maimed. Shrapnel
stays.
Life won't be the same.

Fade Slow

Shouts and screams fade slow.
Hyper-vigilance is real.
This is your life now.

Blackness

Blackness-covered room,
Slight changes in the four five
Avoid suicide.

Time

What is real isn't.
What isn't real is the truth.
Time teaches us this.

BOOK 2

★

My Rifle

When I got your number, I
memorized it instantly,
Forever looking forward to
that first trigger pull.
Everything about you I was
attracted to—
The R.O.F., iron sights, and the
way you felt in my hands.
At first touch I fell in love with
the cold alloy,
Learning you inside and out, I
was overjoyed.
Knowing I'll never forget all
that I've learned.
Even after so many trigger
pulls, you always performed.

Fly Out

Fly out to meet up.
Early morning Osprey flight,
Entering the fight.

Adventures

Adventure lies ahead for us,
The world's greatest young
men:
Long days that are hot and
hostile.
The weight we carry is
colossal.
We rarely sleep in
anticipation,
Yearning for days patrolling
unshaven.

A Warm Welcome

I'm running out of the Osprey
at 0430 in the morning, a full
combat load and all my gear for
the next few months. It weighs
me down, but the challenge is
outweighed by my eagerness
to fight. We've arrived.

It's February 2010, and
I've just landed at a small base
a few clicks outside of the Taliban's
stronghold, named Marjah. It's a
grid-structured city, with north-
south and east-west roads
throughout it, and completely
filled with opium-pushing Taliban.

Marjah is a drug-fueled city in the Helmand province, known for its resistance against foreign invaders and for its key geographic location. Marjah was a key offensive in Operation Enduring Freedom. Named Operation Mostarak, it was aimed at reclaiming the city from Taliban control.

As I make my way across the base, the bird flies away as the commotion settles across the L.Z. and the immediate areas near it. My mind is racing. It's processing so many scenarios that could happen here. This is my first deployment, and I'm actually happy to have finally made my way over here.

The infantry Marines are scattered in their two-man tents or in sleeping holes for one, across the base. It looks like a platoon. I shattered my shoulder thirteen months prior to this, and I was in reconstructive shoulder surgery the day this platoon initially left. Now I show up not having lived with, not having trained with, not really knowing anyone here. I had raised my hand to volunteer as a replacement because I was healed and I was ready to fight.

The walk is long and tiresome, it being this early in the morning, but my mind still races, so the exhaustion is subdued.

I can finally see the route clearance trucks, a few MRAP gun trucks, the Buffalo, a Wrecker, a couple of huskies, and finally the tent. The trucks are all parked and organized in a makeshift sandbag parking lot.

As I walk over to the entrance of the tent, it's quiet

here, and still only 0440, so all the Marines are passed out. Seeing an open cot down the line on the right side all the way near the back of the tent, I head to claim my new home.

I drop my gear on the cot and walk back outside the tent to explore the surrounding area. Within moments I find the piss tubes, the shitter stalls, and a mock I.E.D. lane used to train Marines on local I.E.D. emplacements and types of I.E.D.s in the area.

We are route clearance, and no matter how good I feel about being in the fight with my brothers, it weighs on me that we are here to find bombs. These bombs are concealed everywhere. They're intended to harm us or kill us. It's an eerie feeling that never really goes away. You more or less just accept it and accept your fate.

After about an hour and a half, the Marines of RCP2 start to wake up and begin their day. Unexpectedly, some of the first Marines I see are Marines I actually know. LCPL Cotton and CPL Tubbs walk out to smoke cigarettes but notice me before they begin.

LCPL Lafe Cotton was a great combat Marine—a shorter guy from Michigan who was a real scrapper. He loved confrontation. He would get you going just to see if you would fight him. The perfect type of Marine you want invading a Taliban stronghold. Over the next year, I would become close to Cotton, as he would be my .50 Gunner on our next deployment—one of the best gunners I've seen operate a .50 in combat. Cotton was a great Marine all around in my eyes and a true warrior.

CPL Ernest "Buddy" Tubbs had a similar attitude to LCPL Cotton, very carefree and loose, though he could snap at any moment. He, too, was a fighter. He was from Maryland, where he was raised outdoors, hunting and fishing. CPL Tubbs was one of the best I.E.D. hunters I've ever known. He would go on to find eighty or more I.E.D.s in Sangin Valley roughly a year later. He let his finds define him, and his finds were steep.

"Holy fuck, its Eggen! What the fuck is he doing here?" Cotton said to Tubbs, chuckling, with an unlit cigarette hanging out of his mouth.

Tubbs laughed. "Yeah, Eggen. What are you doing here?"

"I'm one of the replacements," I said.

"Fuck, yes!"

"That's awesome!"

They both spoke at the same time.

"Hey, man, did you pick up any cigarettes? We've been smoking these bullshit L&M's," Cotton asks without hesitation.

Luckily for him and Tubbs, I'd gotten a good tip from one of the older Marines back in the States, which was to buy as many cigarette cartons as I could from the Dwyer PX and sell them to the Marines. That's exactly what I did. Before I left Dwyer, I'd bought three cartons of Newports.

"I actually have three cartons of Newports," I tell them both.

"Get the fuck out of here!" Tubbs responds in disbelief.

"I'll sell you each a carton."
I say.

They both pull fat wads
of cash out of their pockets, and
each hands me money for the
smokes they've just purchased.
"Damn, Eggen, we're glad you're
here," Cotton says

"Yeah, we are," Tubbs adds
in while breaking his L&M
cigarette in half.

They follow me into the
tent and to my cot; I grab my
daypack and pull out the cartons,
handing them to their new
owners.

"Here you go. I'm glad I
could be of service," I say.
"Thanks, Eggen," they both
say as they head outside.
"Welcome to Afghanistan,
brother!" Tubbs says over his
shoulder, walking away to
go smoke his American tobacco with

Cotton. I've been here a short amount of time, and I already feel at home with these disgruntled Marines.

More Marines start to get up, and that's when I make my way out of the tent to the piss tubes. Walking back from the head, I see one of the Marines I knew and was close with before the deployment, SGT Matisi.

Patrick Matisi was born and raised in Chicago, he was a unique individual: For starters, he was older than most Marines. Where most Marines enlist between the ages of eighteen and twenty-two, he was twenty-nine when he enlisted and by this time is thirty-four. He lived many lives in his twenties, as he would later explain to me the importance of youth and living while you're young.

He had colorful, distinctive tattoos that were actually great pieces of art. For some reason, he liked me. He told me I resembled his brother, whom he had rarely seen in recent years. I always took it as a compliment as he seemed to be the guy you want to know. People looked to him for answers.

It could've been because he was older and more mature than everyone, but I believed the real reason was that he actually knew his shit and made good calls under pressure. He was a great leader.

He was shot through his arm and out his chest a little over a year later in Sangin Valley while sweeping a rooftop. He and I are still very close to this day.

"Ha! Eggen is here! You're my new .50 gunner!" he says and

laughs, almost in shock that I actually made it out here.

"I know! They needed replacements, and I volunteered, so here I am."

"Well Eggen..." he pauses. "You're over in our truck." He points to the farthest gun truck from us.

"Its call sign is 'The Fallen.' Go make yourself confortable. I'll send CPL Wade over there to go over the .50 with you," SGT Matisi says as he walks away toward the tent. I start heading toward the truck.

After climbing to the top of the truck, I get into the gun turret; my new home. I start analyzing the .50 and going over the loading and unloading procedures in my mind. Opening and closing the cover group, I run my fingers on top of the bolt, then down the side of the receiver, and ending on the charging handle. This was my gun now.

Out the corner of my eye, I notice a large, dark figure emerge from the tent with a heavy-duty cold weather jacket on. It resembles what looks to be a grizzly bear walking toward me. I know this is a person, but my mind can't help but imagine it's a large grizzly closing in. The grizzly bear stops in his tracks and then looks up at me from under his hood. "Hey, you Eggen?" he asks as he sparks his cigarette.

"Yes, I am."

"Good. I'm CPL Wade, and I'm going to teach you everything you need to know about that machine gun. You'll be able to safely and properly operate this weapon effectively when I'm done with ya" he says with enthusiasm.

Kyle Wade really did remind me of a grizzly bear the first time I ever met him, and I'll never forget that. He was another genuine hard fuck. He knew the inside and outside of every single automatic weapon we had available. His personality was larger than life, and he always was in a good mood, especially when we were deployed.

Machine guns were his bread and butter. He was the best machine gunner in our platoon and was the resident expert on the material. He taught LCPL Cotton everything he knows.

After a few hours of disassembly, assembly, loading, unloading/clearing, malfunctions checks, head-space-timing rituals, and bullshit banter, I absorbed as

much as one person could. I was
exhausted to say the least. CPL
Wade was wide-awake, never
letting up for a moment as he
passed the reins of his baby into
my hands. It was a mantle I didn't
know if I could live up to. CPL
Wade's expectations were high,
and I was brand new.

A couple of days later we
were in the middle of Marjah,
fully engaged in our jobs and the
mission.

"The Fallen", our beloved Gun Truck
in Marjah, early 2010

LCPL Cotton in Marjah, 2010

LCPL Cotton, 2011

CPL Tubbs in Marjah, 2010

SGT Matisi standing next to "The Fallen"
after a 125lb I.E.D. blast, Garmsir 2009

SGT Matisi in Sangin Valley, 2011

CPL Wade with one of his favorite toys,
the 249 S.A.W., Marjah 2010

CPL Tubbs and CPL Wade, 2010

The Author taking a break after a mission, Marjah 2010

We Arrive

We fly for hours.
We prepare for months and
 months.
We arrive to fight.

☺

Bangalores
TNT
C4
H.M.E.
UXO
Dynamite.
Oh
What
A
Sight.

Dangerous Game

Elements are fierce.
Dangerous game we play here,
Fighting against death.

Yesterday the Sun Came Up

Yesterday the sun came up,
Not like the day before.
Yesterday it came up faster,
With so much more.

Baking our skin under our frog
tops,
Swinging sticks that aren't
even on.
I.E.D. after I.E.D.,
No water from the C.O.C.,
The list could go on and on.

Most days it's hard to think
about home,
Knowing I'll never see my
friends,
And leaving my family alone.
So I focus on my boys,
Making sure we're all prepped
for the next mission,
Cleaning our fully automatic
toys.

The Taliban is going to come
back in full force,
Making a ton of noise,
But were trained killing
machines,
A/k/a Marines,
With a shit ton of poise.

White lamp cord or copper
wire,
yellow jugs and pressure
plates,
Add some H.M.E., and it's
a deadly combination that
makes the earth shake.
Find one of these,
You'll be stressed the fuck out.
Stress is a feeling
The dead must leave out.
So embrace the inevitable loss
that you will undergo,
And you'll succeed in an
environment that's meant to
take your soul.

New Traps

Sun crests over hills,
Illuminating our path
Littered with new traps.

0400

Coffee is black mud.
       Early risers get ready.
Prepping is steady.

We Triumph

The days are too long.
The enemy is too close.
We triumph with loss.

Belt-Fed Tongues

Buddy rush and talking guns.
The 240s speak in belt fed
tongues.

Marines fire grenades in the air.
Triggers are pulled, and hate is
shared.

Dirty as hell with facial hair,
We move through fields without a
care.

Taking contact as we press on,
Each compound we find the
enemy is gone.

Leaving behind a trail of bombs,
Pressure plates and batteries, we
call up on COMM.

Under Stress

Seasoned veterans
In salt covered uniforms
Perform under stress.

Never

You sweep left, sweep right
Running low on batteries...
       Never sweep at night.

Up Guns

MRAPs and up guns,
Fifty-cals and two-forties...
We will be ready.

Far Away

Home is far away
In my thoughts and in distance.
Foes stay persistent.

Confusion

Dust fills the air fast.
The mine-roller is now gone.
Confusion turns on.

He's Gone

Death is swift, pink mist.
Where is he? Where did he go?
He's gone with his soul.

Refuge

Inside the wire,
    Troops take refuge from the
        fight.
        Mortars fly at night.

The Storm

The clouds are dark and vast, violently rolling over the landscape, canvassing over anything and everything that is seen. Thunder so deep and terrifying, it's like a monster in the sky, released by Mother Nature to destroy all in its path.

I turn to see the storm as thunder clashes and makes me jump. The lightning, wind, hail, and moon dust ferociously colliding in the air, charging directly toward us at an alarming rate.

Everyone moves into action, finding their purpose as the storm slowly makes its way closer to our position. A group of ten set out to stabilize the tent outside as the winds nearly collapse it. My .50 is up on the truck left out there alone, about to be blasted by the storm. The poncho covering won't hold. My only thought now is to get to my gun before it gets damaged, and take it down. If it's damaged, I cannot perform.

I run as fast as I can toward my truck. Everyone is doing their part with their gear and vehicles as I run past them,urgently sprinting toward The Fallen. The clouds are approaching faster. I have to move quicker.

The back doors are slightly open as I arrive at the truck. "Close those doors!" SGT Matisi shouts from the V.C. seat as I close and lock the doors behind me. Once inside, I move to the gunner's stand and put my head in between the two front seats

"I need to get the .50 down quickly, so I'll need some help passing it down, if you don't mind." I direct my words at LCPL Gray, who nods in agreement as he keeps jamming to "Riders on the Storm" by The Doors.

LCPL Jake "Gary" Gray was the driver of our beloved truck, and one of the best drivers of any vehicle I've seen. Born in northern Idaho he used to race motocross professionally before he joined the Marines and was also a talented drummer. LCPL Gray loved the outdoors and had a deep, genuine love for the Marine Corps. Since both of us were LCPLs in the truck, we shared many responsibilities together, and we grew to be very close friends, remaining so even to this day.

I make my way to the gun turret and as I'm climbing out of it I can see the up guns being removed on each truck like a domino effect. MRAP doors, turret hatches, the buffalo closing up, and more sandbags are being thrown onto the tie-down points of the tent. Everyone is busy. Once out on top of the truck, I can see the storm with more clarity.

The lightning bounces off each cloud, striking the ground like a scorpion's tail attacking its prey, pulling the massive storm behind it. The storm rolls over everything like a tidal wave, hitting an unexpected beach, relentless and consuming. I unscrew the barrel of the gun, and simultaneously a large gust of wind, dirt, and hail hits me like a train; it's here. The dust fills the air instantly, and I can barely see the gun in front of my face. The mixture of hail clanking into the truck and SGT Matisi shouting to hurry up isn't a pleasant sound. The adrenaline activates and moves me faster. My brain works smoother. The painful sensation of hail and dirt intercepting my skin stings like a million wasps.

The barrel is off as I move to the turret and pass it down to LCPL Gray. There is moon dust in every crevice of my body. Next is the receiver, and this has to be fast because the storm is here, and every moment is a thousand moments. Each second is a nightmare on top of this truck as I start releasing the pins in the gun mount, freeing the receiver.

I repeat the same process of passing it down to LCPL Gray.

Fully engulfed by this storm on top of the truck, I briefly pause and embrace the pain and beauty that our planet is throwing at us.

Never dirtier, I climb back into the truck, closing the gunner hatch behind me. Coughing as I enter the truck, I try to release the moon dust within my lungs. Relief overwhelms my body and mind as the sand is no longer blasting me while hail pelts my skin. I gather myself for a few short moments before moving off the gunner's stand. I move to the back seat closest to the back doors, directly across from the rear a/c vent, to gather new air.

As I'm getting comfortable, SGT Matisi and LCPL Gray set up the portable chair in between themselves with the laptop on top of it. "Riders on the Storm" ends, and LCPL Gray connects the laptop to the speakers we have set up in the truck, a makeshift surround-sound system, which actually makes for a very pleasant movie theater.

The wind travels through the MRAP door gaps in a ghoulish manner as the movie starts. Outside the truck, it looks like a foreign planet, orange and red moon dust whipping everywhere as hail breaks on the vehicle.

As I'm looking out the window, I notice something in the distance: It's a Marine. There is a Marine out in the middle of this storm, with his arms out and his eyes shut, stumbling around. I take the .50 receiver off my lap and move it to the gunner's stand, reaching back and unlocking the doors. I crack them slightly.

"Come to my voice!" I yell out the door. He turns his head

toward me like a dog hearing a whistle, turns his body, and starts stumbling toward our truck.

"Come to my voice!" I shout again through the storm, reassuring him of my position. "You're almost here!" I yell one last time. I soon realize as the Marine gets closer that it's CPL Stevens.

CPL Jarren Stevens is from Jacksonville, Florida and could rival CPL Tubbs as the best I.E.D. hunter I know. Stevens had one of the best attitudes I've ever come across overseas. He loved life and was always positive toward everyone. He was a very skilled I.E.D. hunter and a very good Marine to have on your six on patrol, Stevens knew his shit. He was also one of the funnier Marines I've ever come across, just a pure goofball. Nothing seemed to faze his positive outlook. We would become close friends over that deployment.

CPL Stevens realizes how close he is to the back of The Fallen, and he quickly seizes that opportunity to lunge inside. No matter how fast he tries to get inside, the dust has made its way into every corner and pocket of the truck. Luckily for me I had only just started cleaning my gun.

"So, dude, how the fuck did you end up out there?" I ask him.

"Funny story," he starts off, catching his breath. "I went to take a piss over at the piss tubes, and when I finished, I turned around to this fucking storm coming at me." He laughs, telling me the story. The two up front listen in to his story and laugh with us about CPL Stevens getting caught in the storm longer than anyone would want.

I take a moment to really look around and absorb what is happening around me, a beautiful moment for all of us. When you do route clearance you live out of your truck, our truck was family. Within this paralyzing storm we find laughter and solace in each other. We are not concerned about the dirt on our skin or the devastating storm surrounding us. We are happy to be with each other. We relax, and for once Mother Nature is keeping us within the wire for the night. She is giving us a break from the I.E.D.s, IDF, S.A.F., and relentless potshots. All of us enjoy our personal movie theater as the storm outside fails to harness our attention.

LCPL Gray, Marjah 2010

CPL Stevens, Marjah 2010

The Author and CPL Stevens in "The Fallen"
acting upset about the photo SGT Matisi is taking
before that days' mission, Marjah 2010

The crew of "The Fallen", sitting back, about to watch
a movie in our personal movie theater.
CPL Stevens never could keep a straight face, Marjah 2010

BOOK 3

★

Despair

Despair is found here.
The eyes of death are seen
  there.
     Life is nowhere near.

Compassion Lost

Our packs are heavy, but we
don't complain,
Patrolling through marijuana
fields, all types of strains.
Forever we fight, strong and
resilient.
You'd be surprised that our
enemies are brilliant.
Building new bombs every
single day.
Emplacing them in all the
pathways,
Forever adapting to our
tactics—
We find their bombs with
months and months of
practice.
We train our eyes, and our
eyes don't deceive.

So when you find something,
you don't disbelieve.
You go with your instincts to
stay alive...
In this dangerous game it's the
only way to survive.
Once you've become
complacent, you're lost.
You're useless to everyone-
you've become soft.
Marines here are hard
chargers who fight for fun.
We're fierce Devil Dogs who
refuse to get overrun.
Taking the fight to the enemy
relentlessly,
Decisions are always right,
incidentally.
In combat there is no
questioning,
Only actions.
Over time you lose all
compassion.

Preparation for Battle

Prayer music speaks soft.
Preparation for battle—
Marines clean rifles.

Goon

Sangin sun rises.
Enemy advancements soon—
Go condition goon.

Marines At Your Six

Hate fills your soul up.
Losing friends weekly is rough.
We are scared, not tough

Daily adventures
Outside the wire in haste,
Up guns laying waste.

Marines at your six,
Fighting for their freedom here,
Fighters disappear,

Return to their homes,
Farming nonstop as time goes,
Trading AKs for tools.

Overhead

Rounds snap overhead.
Marines bleed, and wounds get
aid.
Nine-line for the dead.

Weeks

Kevlar sweat fills hair,
Dirt under nails and in
cracks—
No showers for weeks

War

War is not joyous.
War is fierce; it is unknown.
War is unbiased.

Not Today

It's so loud I forget who I am. I can't feel anything; I can't hear anything. I try to open my eyes. I cannot see anything; my body is in shock.

"Not today."

Something loud has happened, something abrupt. My life will never be the same. I know that instantly. What has happened? Where am I? Why am I here? What the fuck is happening?

"Not today."

You will not meet Death today. Not today, not tomorrow. You

may go through loss. You will see
horrors... but you will not
experience Death....

"Not today."

I gather myself.
I'm standing two meters away
from the blast site. I look around
the area. I feel the sun, I smell the
air, I see my boys...

Not today, Motherfucker

Our Eyes

Metal detectors'
Batteries always run low.
Our eyes find the prize.

Carefully Follow

Carefully follow.
Step after step, tread lightly.
Pink mist moved slightly.

Upsetting Our Opponents

I.E.D. is a three-letter acronym that
stands for Improvised Explosive
Device.
They're meant to harm and maim
anyone near the blast site

It's hard to find these bombs in
yellow jugs.
This country makes its money
selling drugs.

Small deviations in the dirt, we spot
them as we walk,
Pulling them out of the ground, most
would be in shock

We stay calm as we find these I.E.D.
components.
The more we find, we keep pushing,
Upsetting our opponents.

Facing Death

Marines don't sleep long.
We arise to meet the storm.
Facing death, we fight.

IDF

The whistle comes in:
Dirt, shrapnel, rocks,
percussion.
Life changed from above.

Outside the Wire

Outside the wire is where you'll
find us, we few, the valiant.

Long patrols with even longer
days,
Forever being stuck in this
combat haze.
Every single step, I might
meet death,
Or every corner I turn could
hold my last breath.
You never know what these
days hold—
All you know is fortune favors
the bold.
Cleverly disguised bombs we
spot and take a knee,

Pulling them out of the
ground, filled with HME.

Outside the wire is where
you'll find us,
Tired, exhausted, and covered
in moon dust.
Condition one is how we
patrol,
Lined up in a ranger file with
positive trigger control.
We take contact throughout
the day,
Getting into T.I.C.s and our—
wounded fly away.
Most of us try to stay uplifted
and happy,
As we become increasingly
exhausted patrolling through
this poppy.

Outside the wire is where you'll
find us,
Never knowing peace,
Just foreign warriors
patrolling these streets.
The people appreciate that
you're there.
You can tell by their hateful,
emotionless glare.
They do not care if we are here
or not.
They just want to farm, and
pray they don't get shot.
Taliban uses fear tactics to
keep people in line,
all being killed for talking to
the other side.

Outside the wire is where you'll
find us, we few, the violent.

Out Of Sight

Days are hot and bright.
Enemies stay within reach,
Always out of sight.

Step Off

Each day we step off,
Pushing farther and farther,
Green-zone and gun-fights.

Some Days

Some days here are fun...
Fatigue sets in hourly;
Showers are monthly.

Move Fast

Acts in war are swift.
Hesitate and you will die.
Move fast, stay alive.

Our Opponent Is Fierce

Cold curves rest within my
index finger,
Safety, single shot, and burst
under my thumb linger.
The trigger resets after every
pull,
shoulders receiving recoils
from the tool.

There is no weapon here, only
my brain.
The tool in my hands is meant
to tame
The Communist party and
terrorists alike.
Round after round spewing at
the sight.

Our opponent is fierce and
trivialized.
We won't stop until either one
of us demise.
Combat fills the fields and the
streets.
Slow, steady trigger squeeze as
elite athletes.

HeDp

Forty mike mike fly
Revolutions in the air.
High explosive hits.

Dual purpose,
Annihilating all near,
Castrating all fears.

Enemy fighters
Eliminated quickly.
We do this daily.

Nothing

Ages of battle—
This land knows nothing but
this.
Change wont happen here.

The Insane

Each day comes with sun.
Our rifles are cleaned daily.
The insane find fun.

Everything Is Smooth

The violence nests in my brain,
Manifesting its way into my
soul,
Applying violence as a tool.
Everything is slow.
Everything is smooth.

Pride

Young men in their prime
Came to fight this war and
die—
Honor filled with pride.

Solace

Afghani bear dogs,
Late nights around the fire—
Marines find solace.

Coffee

The dream I am having is interrupted, my hammock shakes, and Gunny is standing over me. "Eggen, wake up and make me some coffee," he says as he starts casually walking away. I barely have my eyes open, and coffee doesn't sound like the worst drink for once.

Gunnery Sergeant Corey Wodrich was our platoon sergeant on my second deployment. He loved his troops, but I think he loved his coffee even more. He'd been a Marine since before 9/11 and was sent to Afghanistan back in 2002. He often reminded us that this place hasn't changed in the last nine years.

Gunny was a good Marine and loved the Marine Corps when it wasn't being ruined by political bullshit. He made great calls and let us do our jobs the right way. He was the best platoon sergeant I ever had.

It's 0400, and the sun hasn't even broken the horizon. It's still pitch black outside. The air is cold, being this close to the base of the mountains. I unzip my sleeping system and begin to make my way out of it, slowly. I turn my body and swing my legs out of my hammock and rest my feet on top of my boots. As I start putting my feet into my boots, I begin to hear the infantry Marines sending mortars off to engage the enemy. The sound is one you never forget, the round sliding down the mortar tube, then the thud of the round hitting the bottom, followed by an explosive THOOMP as it flies into the night sky. It's like a beautiful symphony.

I rub my eyes as I'm walking to the back of the truck, 'Faded Line', to find this coffee, French press, and water heater. The water heater was passed down to us from the platoon we replaced. The French press and coffee grounds are all mailed out to us from back home. I search briefly as I find the coffee grounds in a large zip-lock bag, right next to the French press in the back seat.

The problem with me making coffee for Gunny is that I've never actually had coffee before or brewed it before. It's something I've actively avoided in my life because to me it tastes like shit, or at least I always assumed it did. Today will be my first time trying coffee. I know that instantly as I break open the zip-lock bag full of powdered coffee grounds. I inhale the most beautiful scent that has ever passed through my nose.

My mind craves this coffee now. I empty three water bottles into the water heater and prep the French press for use. The water boils surprisingly fast. I unplug it and pour it over the coffee in the press. The mixture of coffee grounds and steaming water is a magical change from this country. Afghanistan smells like burning trash, expended rounds, burning shit, and death. The new coffee scent is filling my nose and lungs as my attitude toward this drink changes.

The night is still cold and slightly wet on the ground, and

the base is quiet—no one is awake
other than the two mortar teams
in the corner of the base, still
consistently firing rounds.

It is partially the
circumstances I am in at this
moment that have made me crave
this coffee so strongly, and
partially the organic purity that
is this black coffee. This is a clean and
pure energy drink, unlike the
corn syrup-filled ones we get. The
warmth is commanding in this
cold area—the smell of the warm
coffee consumes me.

"That coffee done yet,
Eggen?" Gunny asks as he walks
up to me, coming from the
Buffalo. He sees me entranced by
the coffee.

"Uhh, yeah, Gunny. It's
almost done," I say. I make my
way to the V.C. seat and grab my
daypack to search for my canteen

cup, so I can drink this shit as soon as possible. I find the cup with enthusiasm and head back to the rear of 'Faded Line'. Gunny is standing there, pouring himself the first cup of many throughout the day. The coffee is thick, black as the night, and mud-like as he pours it. He finishes his cup, grabs my canteen cup from me, and starts pouring the black gold into my cup. He hands it back to me and then cheers me, and cracks his Gunny smile.

Not only am I about to embark on the first taste of black coffee, but I am in the middle of a combat zone, surrounded by hopelessness and death. To come across something for the first time and have it be something positive over here is rare.

The mortar teams are echoing in the background.

"Eggen, let's go watch those Marines fuck up the bad guys with those rounds." Gunny says and motions for me to follow him.

He starts walking toward the sound of the mortars, and I walk with him. The coffee is too hot to actually taste or drink it, but I've become increasingly impatient as it sits in front of me, begging me to drink it down. The cool air seems to be affecting the scalding beverage within my canteen cup. Knowing it's getting cooler and cooler, my patience thins out.

We arrive at the mortar teams in the southeast corner of the base just as they send two more rounds off. The rounds fly across the battlefield, and you can hear them hitting and detonating in the distance. It's a beautiful display of American firepower as these young men send hate and discontent in indirect fire form.

These men—barely old enough to vote—are sending rounds hurtling toward the Taliban with fierce accuracy. The area is so dark, the only light we can see comes from the mortar tube tips as the rounds explode out. We sit watching and waiting for our coffee to cool down.

At this point the coffee is cool enough to drink with the cool air chilling our canteen cups. I bring the canteen cup to my lips and take a large breath of the coffee aroma.

When I first drink the coffee, it's hot, still, as it hits my lips. It's bitter and tastes unlike anything I've ever had up until that point. There is no sugar; there is no cream— it's black, it's sludge, and it's perfect.

We sit there at 0420, watching the mortar teams demolish enemies across the field, enjoying our beautiful drinks. It is one of the most memorable moments for me in life. I have found something I love in the middle of this shit hole. Something so profound in my life at that point is amazing. I have found a unique love for coffee. Sitting in the middle of the Green-Zone, life is sacred.

Life is rare here in war. New, happy things are rare, and death is common, as is despair.

Gunny never was fond of pictures, Sangin 2011

The Author at PB Alcatraz spring 2011

SSP Bounty Hunter, Helmand 2009

SSP Bounty Hunter, Helmand 2009

Patrolling in Marjah 2010

I.E.D. strike on the Buffalo, Sangin 2011

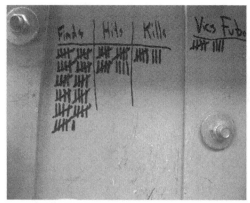

RCP2 Finds/Strikes List, Sangin 2011

Glossary of Terms

C.O.C – Combat Operations Center
COMM – Communications
H.M.E. – Homemade Explosive
IDF – Indirect Fire
I.E.D. – Improvised Explosive Device
L.Z. – Landing Zone
PX – Personnel Exchange
RCP – Route Clearance Platoon
R.O.F. – Rate of Fire
S.A.F. – Small Arms Fire
T.I.C. – Troops in Contact
UXO – Unexploded Ordnance
V.C. – Vehicle Commander
MRAP - Mine Resistant Ambush Protected Vehicle
BUFFALO - a truck, created by Force Protection. It has a mechanical retractable arm with a claw on the tip of it, designed to investigate I.E.D.s. etc.
V-22 Osprey – a Boeing American multi-mission, tilt-rotor military aircraft with both vertical takeoff and landing, and short takeoff and landing capabilities.

Acknowledgments

This book wouldn't have happened without the love and support from, my mother, father, Keith Honkala, Trish Faller, Grandpa Hatcher, Preston 'Sleepe12' Young, Robert Hatcher and Family, Mariah Lavon Cates, the Khanals, Evan Durham, James Bell and Georgia, Nate Campbell, Patrick Matisi and family, Jake 'Gary' Gray, Jake Daily, Mike Maniglia and family, Johnny Fried, Bryan Fried, Mike Yanchura and family, Griffith, Matt Hudson, John White, Ernest 'Buddy' Tubbs and family, Kyle Wade, Mateo Taylor, Andre Forrest, Kevin Blair, Ben Works, Boo the Destoyer of Negativity, Dylan Sheehan, Jeff DeYoung and Cena, Brendan Marzan and family, Brandon Pressley, Lafe Cotton, Jarren Stevens and family, Randy Davis, Matthew Dawson and family, Patrick Fulco and family, Nick Fulco, Dave Bobrowsky and family, Eli the Barber, J.J. Eggen, Mike Heck, Luke Hamilton,

Corey Wodrich, Dennis 'Lil D' Wright, Jake
Lutz, Chase 'Country' Calverly, Matthew Tate,
Brandon 'Speedy' Edwards, Leonard Angel
and Family, Kevin Hostetler and family,
Hugh Farr, Michael Urrutia, Shawn "1stSgt"
Martin, Alexander Bedenbaugh, Rollie
Lemons, Marty Ryan, The Marines of RCP2,
The Marines of MAC who supported me
throughout my time there, The United States
Marine Corps, Palm Beach County and the
beautiful state of Florida, and finally to
everyone who has ever supported me from
past or present, I thank you forever!

About the Author

Justin Thomas Eggen was born March 28th, 1989 in West Palm Beach, Florida. Once out of high school, in summer 2007, he spent nearly the next full year seeking a challenge.

In early 2008 he enlisted with the U.S. Marine Corps, and on Mother's Day he shipped off for Parris Island. He earned the title "United States Marine" on August 8th 2008, continued on to Marine Combat Training, and finally graduated Combat Engineer School in November.

He was assigned to 2nd Combat Engineer Battalion, but within one month he shattered his right shoulder in a very pointless physical training evolution. Thirteen months later, and after reconstructive surgery, he found himself on the front lines of our nation's battlefields.

In February 2010 he arrived at Route Clearance Platoon 2 and operated out of Marjah, Afghanistan for the next four months. In April 2011, he found himself on the front lines again with RCP2, pushing into Sangin Valley, Afghanistan.

In May 2012, the author was released from active duty Marine Corps as a Sergeant of Marines.

He now lives in his hometown of West Palm Beach and focuses on upcoming literary works, traveling, surfing, hiking, skimboarding, scuba diving, and enjoying the outdoors not looking for I.E.D.s.

The Author in 2014, on his Harley

COMING SOON:

'Outside The Wire: a U.S. Marine's
Collection of Combat Poems and
Short Stories Volume 2'

&

'Love/Hate/Life/Death
A Collection of Poetry
By
Salty Sea Shaman'

"Untitled" 1st Page Artwork by
Matt Hudson
@hudsonfineart

www.outsidethewirebook.com

FB & IG:

@outsidethewirebook

Email:

outsidethewirebook@gmail.com

Made in the USA
Columbia, SC
28 April 2019